GREAT EXPLORATIONS

FRANCISCO CORONADO

GREAT EXPLORATIONS

FRANCISCO CORONADO

In Search of the Seven Cities of Gold

STEVEN OTFINOSKI

BENCHMARK BOOKS

MARSHALL CAVENDISH
NEW YORK

With special thanks to Professor Stephen Pitti, Yale University,
for his careful reading of this manuscript.

Benchmark Books
Marshall Cavendish
99 White Plains Road
Tarrytown, New York 10591-9001

Library of Congress Cataloging-in-Publication Data

Otfinoski, Steven.
Francisco Coronado : in search of the seven cities of gold / by Steven Otfinoski.
v. cm.-(Great explorations)
Includes bibliographical references and index.
Contents: A gentleman of Spain-A new life in the New World-The grandest expedition-The battle of Cibola-Lands
of wonders- Trouble at Tiguex-The sea of grass-End of the rainbow-A conquistador's fall-
Francisco Coronado and his times.
ISBN 0-7614-1484-3
1. Coronado, Francisco V,squez de, 1510-1554-Juvenile literature.
2. Explorers-America-Biography-Juvenile literature. 3. Explorers-Spain-Biography-Juvenile literature. 4.
America-Discovery and exploration-Spanish-Juvenile literature. 5. Southwest, New-Discovery and exploration-
Spanish-Juvenile literature. [1. Coronado, Francisco V,squez de, 1510-554. 2. Explorers. 3. Southwest,
New-Discovery and exploration. 4. America-Discovery and exploration-Spanish.] I. Title. II. Series.
E125.V3 O84 2002
979'.01'092-dc21

2002003935

Photo Research by Candlepants Incorporated

Printed in Hong Kong

1   3   5   6   4   2

Contents

Foreword 6

ONE A Gentleman of Spain 8

TWO A New Life in the New World 12

THREE The Grandest Expedition 18

FOUR The Battle of Cibola 24

FIVE Lands of Wonders 32

SIX Trouble at Tiguex 40

SEVEN The Sea of Grass 46

EIGHT TEnd of the Rainbow 50

NINE A Conquistador's Fall 58

Afterword 64

Francisco Coronado and His Times 69

Further Research 70

Bibliography 72

Source Notes 73

Index 75

foreword

The explorers of the 1500s had many strange ideas of what they would find in the New World. Maps of the day had oceans dotted with sea serpents and other mythical beasts. Travel books contained pictures of native peoples who looked like aliens from another planet.

One of the most enduring and intriguing legends about the New World was a country of fabulous wealth. It was called the Seven Cities of Cibola and each city was said to be rich in gold.

This is the story of Francisco Vásquez de Coronado, the bold explorer whose mission it was to find these seven cities for Spain. Coronado seemed destined to become the greatest of the Spanish conquistadores in the New World. But he ended up one of the most dismal failures. At least, that's what people thought at the time.

Coronado found no cities of gold. He discovered no great civiliza-

This famous painting shows Coronado's huge expedition making its way across what is now New Mexico.

tions. However, he and his soldiers discovered something perhaps just as great from the modern—day perspective—the American Southwest.

Coronado's story is one filled with adventure, hardship, wonder, violence, and betrayal. It is a tale of greed, but also one of great courage. Like Christopher Columbus, Coronado went to his grave thinking he was a failure, never realizing that more than four and a half centuries later he would be remembered as one of the great explorers of North America.

ONE

A Gentleman of Spain

From 1492, when Christopher Columbus made his first voyage to the New World, to about 1550, Europe experienced its golden age of exploration. Explorers from England, Portugal, the Netherlands, and France journeyed to Africa, Asia, and the Americas in search of riches, land, and adventure.

No nation benefited more from this great age of exploration than Spain. Daring Spanish explorers known as *conquistadores* carved out an empire in the New World that was the envy of every other European country. This took place with an astonishing swiftness. Only eleven years after Columbus's last voyage in 1502, Vasco Núñez de Balboa crossed the narrow strip of land known as the Isthmus of Panama. He became the first European to gaze on the Pacific Ocean. Just six years later, Hernando Cortés sailed from Cuba to the east coast of a new land—Mexico. There he discovered and conquered the empire of the

Balboa, discoverer of the Pacific, was the first of the Spanish conquistadores. Coronado was one of the last of these bold explorers.

Aztecs. In 1533, Francisco Pizarro conquered another fabulously
wealthy kingdom, that of the Incas in Peru. Two years later, one of
Pizarro's men, Diego de Almagro, explored western Bolivia and Chile,
crossing the mighty Andes Mountains. The silver and gold found in
Mexico and Peru made Spain the wealthiest country in Europe.

Among those young men of Spain who longed to make their way in
the New World was one Francisco Vásquez de Coronado. Coronado
was born about 1510 in Salamanca, an ancient city in west central
Spain. Salamanca had been conquered in 220 B.C. by the mighty general Hannibal of the powerful North African city of Carthage on his way
to attack Rome with an army of elephants. But Salamanca was best

Spain's Golden Century

Some historians say the 1500s were truly Spain's Golden Age. By 1550, it controlled Mexico, Central America, most of western South America, almost all the islands in the West Indies, and a good portion of the present-day southwestern United States. In Africa, Spain possessed the Canary Islands and part of northern Africa.

Charles I, crowned king of Spain in 1516, brought the Netherlands, Burgundy, and Luxembourg—which he already ruled as the duke of Burgundy—into the Spanish Empire. Three years later, he was crowned Holy Roman Emperor, that is, ruler of what was then Germany, and took the second title of Charles V.

Under Charles's son, Philip II, who came to the Spanish throne in 1556, the Spanish century reached its peak. Late in the century, Portugal became united with Spain. The Philippine Islands also came under Spanish control. Spain became the first empire "on which the sun never sets" because it had colonies in both the Eastern and the Western Hemispheres.

Charles I presided over a great empire that stretched from North Africa to the area that became the present-day Southwestern southwestern United States.

known for the world-renowned University of Salamanca, founded in 1218 by King Alfonso IX.

Coronado's family was old and noble, but not wealthy. What money they did have was destined to go to Coronado's eldest brother. This was the age-old custom in Spanish families. Younger sons were expected to make their own way in the world. Most chose to become priests, monks, soldiers, or courtiers or attendants of the royal court.

Coronado chose this last path—at least at first. While at the court of King Charles I, he made a powerful friend in Antonio de Mendoza. Mendoza was a government official and also came from a noble family. He was about twenty years older than Coronado, and some historians believe he may have been a relative. Whatever their connection, Mendoza formed a warm friendship with Coronado and looked on him as his protégé.

In 1535, Mendoza was appointed the first viceroy of New Spain, which is now Mexico. A viceroy was the king's representative in Spanish colonies. Mendoza chose a number of young men to serve as his aides, and among these was twenty-five-year-old Coronado. Coronado was going to the New World, not as a sailor or a soldier of fortune, but as an assistant to the most powerful man in New Spain. Ahead of him lay a great future, far greater than he could have imagined.

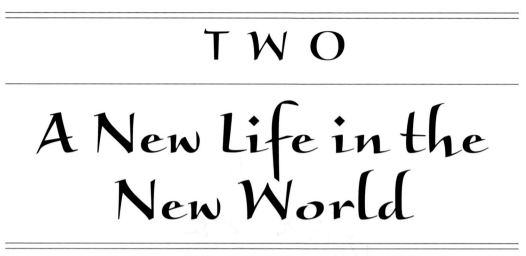

T W O

A New Life in the New World

When Viceroy Mendoza and his team arrived in Mexico City, the capital of New Spain, in 1535, they found it to be the center of a thriving colonial empire. But although the Aztecs and other Native American peoples were subdued, they still were a threat. Poor treatment from some Spaniards had angered many Indians and made them rebellious. One reason Mendoza had been appointed viceroy was to improve relations with the Indians. He was a member of a new breed of Spaniards in the New World. The day of the swashbuckling conquistadores was almost over. Now, sensible administrators were needed who could run this vast empire.

Coronado wasted no time fitting into New Spain society. Within a year of his arrival, he married one of the colony's prize beauties, Beatríz de Estrada. She was the daughter of the deceased royal Spanish treasurer, Alonso de Estrada. Coronado's mother-in-law gave him half of her estate at the time of the marriage.

Antonio de Mendoza was known as the "good viceroy," partly because so many of the other Spanish administrators in the New World were cruel, corrupt, or incompetent.

Mexico City – Capital of New Spain

When conquistador Hernando Cortés conquered the Aztecs in 1521, he almost completely destroyed their capital city, Tenochtitlán. On its ruins he built a new city, Mexico City.

In its earliest days, Mexico City was a hazardous place to live for the Spaniards and their Indian subjects. The valley that surrounded Mexico City was a lake basin without an outlet to the sea. The city would regularly flood in the rainy season and many lives would be lost. The worst flooding occurred in 1629, when thirty thousand people died. After that, the Spanish built a huge canal to carry off the rainwater.

By then, about half of all Spaniards in the Americas lived in either Mexico City or the city of Lima, Peru, to the south. Today, Mexico City is the largest metropolis in the Western Hemisphere.

Hernando Cortés hoped to lead the expedition to find Cibola, but the job went to the younger, more favored Coronado.

Soon after his marriage, Mendoza gave Coronado his first test. He sent him to put down a rebellion of Indians and black slaves at a silver mine. Coronado did so with a minimum of violence. The viceroy rewarded him by appointing him his secretary and closest adviser.

Then in August 1538, the twenty-eight-year-old Coronado was named governor of New Galicia, New Spain's northernmost province. He replaced the corrupt and unpopular governor, Nuño de Guzmán. Guzmán was arrested for his cruel treatment of the Indians and returned to Spain in disgrace. Coronado was the opposite of Guzmán.

This map of New Galicia shows how far Spanish settlement of Mexico had spread in the seventeen years since Cortés conquered the Aztecs.

Coronado's march in search of the Seven Cities of Gold was the first expedition to penetrate the western United States.

He was well liked, handsome, and a competent administrator. With his wife, Coronado started the first charity in the New World, a home for orphaned girls. Coronado was living a comfortable life as governor of New Galicia, but fate soon had other plans for him.

The Spaniards in New Spain had heard rumors of a great empire that lay to the north. This empire was said to be as great and rich as that of the Aztecs and Incas. Instead of one or two great cities, this kingdom was said to have seven. They were called the Seven Cities of Cibola.

Actually, the legend of the Seven Cities had been told for centuries in Europe, but there it was known as the Seven Cities of the Seven Bishops. These bishops, so the legend went, were driven out of Portugal by the Moors, Muslim invaders from Africa. They crossed the ocean and used their great wealth to build seven great cities of gold on a floating island called Antilia in the Atlantic Ocean. Now the question facing Coronado and other Spaniards was, could Antilia be part of the New World? The answer came not from the Indians, who were full of conflicting stories, but from three Spanish conquistadores.

In 1528, Álvar Núñez Cabeza de Vaca was part of an ill-fated Spanish expedition to Florida. After sailing from Florida to Texas and living several years among the people of the Southwest, only Cabeza de Vaca and three others survived. One of them was a Moroccan slave named Estéban. The four men crossed Texas on foot and crossed the Rio Grande into Mexico. They arrived in New Spain in 1536, after walking an incredible one thousand miles. In their eight years of wandering, Cabeza de Vaca and the others lived among different Indian peoples. They heard colorful stories of the Seven Cities of Gold. They even claimed to have seen great stone buildings inlaid with the greenish-blue mineral turquoise and silver.

Viceroy Mendoza heard these stories with great interest. He decided to send his own expedition to confirm what Cabeza de Vaca had seen. Because he did not want to make this seem like a military expedition, Mendoza chose a Franciscan friar to lead the party. Friar Marcos de Niza was a popular and trusted monk who had been with Pizarro in Peru. To guide Marcos, Mendoza sent Estéban, who was now his personal servant. Estéban was big and strong, knew the territory, and had lived among the Indians and knew their ways.

On March 7, 1539, Marcos and his party of friars and Indians set off from New Galicia for parts unknown. In his orders, Mendoza wrote that they were "to note the kind of people. . . . the quality and fertility of the land . . . and the rocks and metals." It was surely the rocks and metals he was most interested in hearing about. For if the Seven Cities were indeed golden, it would be the richest discovery yet made in this strange new world.

THREE

The Grandest Expedition

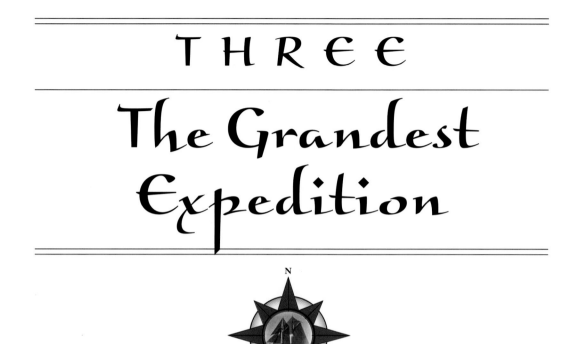

Friar Marcos's party traveled north to a place called Vacapa in northern Mexico. He sent Estéban ahead and waited for word from him. If Estéban found nothing of consequence, he would send back a small cross by Indian messenger. If he found a city, he was to send a large cross. If he found a country greater than New Spain, he was to send back a huge cross.

Four days later an Indian from Estéban's party returned. He brought Friar Marcos a cross the size of a man. Another messenger urged Marcos to come immediately. Marcos was sure he was about to join Estéban in the city of Cibola. The excited friar immediately set off northward and eventually reached what is probably New Mexico.

He had arrived at a high plateau when an Indian from Estéban's party brought shocking news. Estéban, who had entered Cibola, had been taken captive by the Zuni, a Native American people, who lived there. The Zuni were displeased with the way the bold Estéban treated

The proud Zuni were the first Native Americans the Spanish encountered in what was to become the United States.

THE SPANISH MISSIONARIES

It should not be surprising that Viceroy Mendoza entrusted the important mission of exploring Cibola to Friar Marcos. Missionaries were as important in the exploration and settlement of Spanish America as conquistadores and politicians. Every exploring party had at least one missionary who served as its spiritual leader.

The main job of the Spanish missionaries was to convert the Native Americans to the Roman Catholic religion. Nearly as important, the missionaries molded the Indians into obedient Spanish subjects, but subjects with few rights. Early on, missionaries established missions. These were communities where Native Americans could be fed, clothed, and sheltered while they were instructed in the Catholic faith and taught a trade. The missionaries taught the Indians to farm using European methods, raise livestock, and do other kinds of work. They often provided a refuge from the harsh treatment many Indians received from other Spaniards.

The Spanish missionaries' influence reached its peak in the Spanish colony of California under Father Junipero Serra, who established a string of missions there about 230 years after Coronado's expedition.

Perhaps the most famous Spanish missionary in the Americas was Junipero Serra who established a string of nine missions along the California coast before his death in 1784. After that, twelve more missions were built in California. Many of these still stand today as museums and offer a unique view of life in early Spanish America.

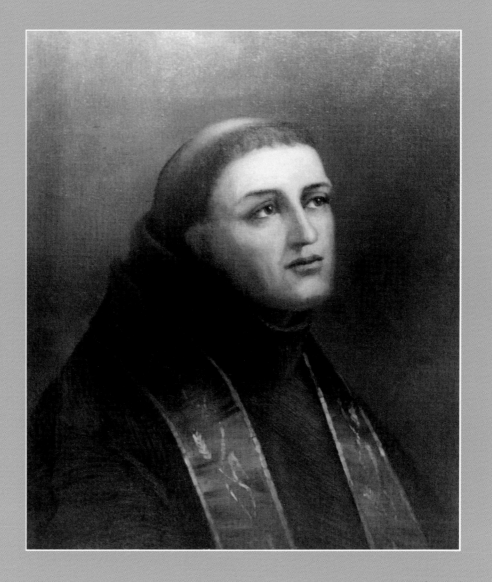

their women. They also believed him to be a spy for the Spanish. The Zuni kept Estéban in a hut for three days and then released him. As Estéban ran for his life, the Zuni shot him down with arrows. The wily explorer who had crossed a continent was dead.

Friar Marcos feared he too would be killed by the Zuni and prepared to flee homeward. But before he did so, he wanted to see the great city that it had been his mission to find. He stood on the plateau and gazed through the dazzling desert sunlight into the distance. "The city from where I beheld it looked splendid," he later wrote." It is certainly the handsomest one I have seen in all these parts. The houses are of stone. As well as I could judge, it is even larger than the city of Mexico."

Before leaving, Friar Marcos marked the spot with a mound of stones and a cross. He named the entire region the New Kingdom of St. Francis after his order's patron saint. On his return journey, he was met by Coronado in New Galicia. The governor accompanied the friar to Mexico City.

Mendoza listened to Friar Marcos's description of Cibola with rapt attention. The friar embellished his report with tales told him by the Indians he met along the way. Cibola, he claimed, not only was rich in turquoise, as Cabeza de Vaca had said, but in gold as well. Gold was everywhere. Here, thought Mendoza, was a land that could make the empires of the Aztecs and the Incas seem puny by comparison.

The viceroy wasted no time in organizing a proper expedition to investigate Cibola and prepare the way for its conquest. His choice to lead the expedition was the trusted and talented governor of New Galicia, Francisco Coronado.

This news was distressing to another conquistador who had also sought this appointment. He was no other than the conqueror of the Aztecs—Hernando Cortés. Cortés yearned for a new challenge to reverse his fortunes. He held the title of marquis and lived on a rich estate, but the king had stripped him of his power. He now realized

Mendoza would never let him lead the expedition to Cibola. So he returned to Spain to complain to the king.

He was never to return to the land he was the first to conquer.

Cortés's loss was Coronado's gain. His expedition to Cibola would be the grandest ever in the New World, far larger than the exploring parties of either Cortés or Pizarro. There were some 230 horsemen, a few of them non-Spanish, sixty-two foot soldiers, and four friars, including Friar Marcos. There were in addition, more than six hundred Indians and black slaves who would manage over one thousand head of cattle, goat, and sheep and one thousand horses. To supplement the meat the animals would provide, there were tons of supplies. Clothing and other necessities were too impractical for the expedition to carry. They were packed aboard three ships under the command of Hernando de Alarcón. These ships were to meet later with the land expedition at the head of the Gulf of California.

F O U R

The Battle of Cibola

The expedition set off in February from Compostela, the capital of New Galicia. From there it marched to Culiacán, the most remote Spanish outpost in New Spain. A young man named Pedro de Castañeda joined the party there. Little is known about Castañeda, but years later, he wrote a detailed account of the expedition that has been invaluable to historians.

"There were so many men of such high quality among the Spaniards, that such a noble body was never collected in the Indies," Castañeda wrote. Then he added, more darkly, "Had he [Coronado] paid more attention and regard to the position in which he was placed . . . things would not have turned out as they did."

Such an observation could only have been made in retrospect. As the dashing General Coronado set off, his armor gleaming in the sunlight and colors flying, all things seemed possible.

Coronado cuts a bold and dashing figure as he prepares to lead the largest Spanish expedition ever mounted in the New World. To his right is one of the ever-present friars who accompanied him.

At Culiacán, Coronado took a smaller party of seventy-five horsemen, twenty-five to thirty foot soldiers, and several Indian allies, and pushed on to Cibola. Friar Marcos went with them. Tristán de Arellano was left in charge of the main force. The road to Cibola was a long and difficult one. They reached the border of the present-day United States, crossed into Arizona, and on May 26, 1540, entered the so-called

Valley of Hearts, named by Cabeza de Vaca. He might have called it that because its cool shadows and plentiful water gave the weary explorer heart to go on.

The Zuni fiercely defended Hawikuh against Coronado's men, but the Spaniards' superior weapons soon overcame them.

The Battle of Cibola

As their food supplies ran low, the men began complaining about the heat and hunger. Coronado had another problem—Friar Marcos. Landmarks were not where the friar said they would be. His sense of

THE ZUNI

It is not surprising that Coronado met resistance from the Zuni at Hawikuh. The Zuni have continued to cling to their way of life in the face of white settlement and culture to this day.

In 1680, after the Pueblo Revolt, the Zuni abandoned their six villages. The present-day pueblo of Zuni, however, was built on the site of one of those seven villages. Today, many Zuni live in the same kind of pueblos their ancestors did. Other Zuni live nearby in modern homes.

Unlike many other Native American peoples, the Zuni have resisted efforts to convert them to Christianity. They have held firm to their religion. Every year between Thanksgiving and early December, the Zuni perform their Shalako ceremony. Dancers wear masks to represent their gods and bless new homes.

This depiction of the Zuni Shalako dance was rendered by contemporary Hopi artist Fred Kabotie.

This spirit of independence also carries over into Zuni public life. In 1970, they became the first Native American people to run their own social programs as set up by the Bureau of Indian Affairs.

distance was inaccurate. The general was beginning to wonder if Friar Marcos wasn't wrong about the other things that he told the viceroy about Cibola.

On June 23, they entered a desert region in what is now Arizona, southeast of Tucson. A number of horses died from heat exhaustion and a soldier and two Indians perished after eating a poisonous plant, called "water hemlock" by later travelers. The others persevered and soon entered a green, fertile area in western New Mexico near the present-day city of Gallup. They arrived at the same plateau where Friar Marcos first laid eyes on Cibola many months earlier. They saw no city of gold but one made of sun-baked mud. Cibola was actually Hawikuh, a Zuni pueblo, or town, made of interconnected apartments. As Castañeda later wrote, "There are haciendas [ranch houses] in New Spain which make a better appearance at a distance."

The only thing that Hawikuh had that the Spaniards wanted was food. The Zuni did not make them welcome. They had killed Estéban, the Moroccan slave, and now they were prepared to kill again to preserve their home from these foreign invaders.

Coronado was reluctant to fight. He had orders to treat the Indians he met with kindness when at all possible, but the Zuni gave him little choice but to defend himself and his men. The musketeers and crossbow men fired and the Indians quickly fled. The Spaniards entered Hawikuh. Again, they met resistance. Coronado himself scaled the wall of a stone house on a ladder. In a long letter to Mendoza, he later described what happened next.

> . . . *they knocked me down to the ground twice with countless great stones which they threw down from above, and if I had not been protected by the very good headpiece which I wore, I think that the outcome would have been bad for me.*

It was bad enough. Coronado had two face wounds, an arrow in his foot, and bruises all over his body. There were no Spanish fatalities, but a number of men were wounded. The Zuni fled, and the Spaniards took over the town. Three days later, the Zuni returned to make peace. They gave Coronado some turquoise. He was impressed, but this was not the gold and silver he had hoped to find. He was generous towards the Indians and offered them the gifts of Christianity and Spanish rule. But the Zuni wanted nothing more to do with the Spaniards. They gathered their belongings and left the next day for the surrounding hills.

Although disappointed, Coronado began to appreciate what the Zuni had achieved. Of their pueblo homes he wrote to Mendoza, "they are very good houses, with three and four and five stories, where there are very good apartments and good rooms with corridors . . ." He also praised their tortillas, or corn cakes, calling them the best he had ever tasted.

Coronado had nothing good to say, however, about Friar Marcos, whom he now considered a fool and a fraud."I can assure you that . . . he has not told the truth in a single thing that he said," he wrote the viceroy." The Seven Cities are seven little villages, all having the kind of houses I have described."

When the rest of the expedition arrived a short time later, their disappointment quickly turned to anger, most of it directed at Friar Marcos. Coronado sent a small party to deliver his letter back to Mendoza. Friar Marcos wisely decided to go with them. If he stayed, he would have had more to fear from the Spaniards than from the Zuni.

As for Coronado, he was disappointed but not defeated. He still had high hopes that more than stone and mud lay beyond the Seven Cities of Cibola. There could well be greater riches further on, or as the Spanish say, "*más allá*." Coronado would now make Cibola his base camp and send others out to explore what lay beyond the Seven Cities.

FIVE

Lands of Wonders

Pedro de Tovar led the first expedition party that Coronado sent out from Hawikuh. Tovar led his men northwest into what is now northern Arizona. After traveling about 160 miles, they arrived at a pueblo at nightfall. In the morning, the inhabitants came out dressed for war. Tovar took them to be Zuni, but they were actually Hopi. Some of the Hopi put down a line of cornmeal across the ground. They warned the Spaniards not to cross it. Tovar had come too far to be threatened this way and his men crossed the line. A brief struggle took place and the Hopi fled. They returned in peace with gifts of corn and piñon nuts. Again, the Spaniards found no gold, but Tovar became intrigued when the Hopi spoke of a great river further west.

Returning to Hawikuh, Tovar told Coronado about the river. The general sent another of his captains, García López de Cárdenas, to look for this river. Coronado may have thought there would be more settle-

Of the many wonders Coronado's captains saw in their far-flung travels, none was more awesome than the Grand Canyon, in what was to become Arizona.

ments along the river. He believed that the river flowed to the Gulf of California. If his men followed its course, they might meet the ships sent north under Alarcón.

Cárdenas and his party of twenty-five followed Tovar's route and in twenty days reached the river. They stood above it on a high rocky place. For three days, the party searched for a path down to the river. Finally, Cárdenas sent three men down at the least difficult place. They returned later that day, unable to reach the river. According to Pedro de Castañeda, Cárdenas had seriously misjudged the depth of the canyon.

THE GRANDEST OF CANYONS

The Grand Canyon existed for six million years before Coronado and his captains arrived on the scene. It was formed by erosion caused by the rushing waters of the Colorado River. The water, aided by rain, wind, and melting snow, carved out the towering canyon walls.

Cárdenas and his men saw the canyon from the South Rim. The North Rim was not discovered until 236 years later. Spanish friar and missionary Francisco Escalante was searching for an overland route from the Spanish stronghold of Santa Fe to Monterey, California, when he stumbled upon it.

The canyon was not fully explored until 1869, when American geologist John Wesley Powell led an expedition down the Colorado River by boat. He named it the Grand Canyon. It was made a national monument in 1908 and became a national park by act of Congress in 1919.

It is regrettable that Cárdenas's report to Coronado on the Grand Canyon was lost. It would be interesting to see what the first Europeans to see it thought of this natural wonder.

The Grand Canyon, which meant little to García López
de Cárdenas, today receives five million visitors a year.

"Those who stayed above had estimated that some huge rocks on the sides of the cliffs seemed to be about as tall as a man," he wrote, "but those who went down swore that when they reached these rocks they were bigger than the great tower of Seville [a city in Spain]."

The comparison of the canyon's depth to the tallest cathedral tower in Spain proved to be an understatement. What Cárdenas was staring into was perhaps the greatest natural wonder in North America—the Grand Canyon of the Colorado River. He and his men were the first Europeans to see it, although they hardly appreciated its grandeur. They saw the Grand Canyon as just one more obstacle in their search for gold and silver. They quickly returned to Hawikuh to make their report. Unfortunately, that report has not survived.

The third expedition from Hawikuh was led by a very different kind of soldier. Melchior Díaz was not of noble birth, as were most of Coronado's officers, but was a commoner. He had been *alcalde*, or mayor, of Culiacán when Cabeza de Vaca and his party returned from their long journey. Díaz knew the northern frontier as well as any Spaniard alive, having been sent to Arizona as Viceroy Mendoza's scout in 1539 to confirm the reports of Friar Marcos.

Coronado now sent him south to the Sonoran Desert to order Arellano to bring the main force to Hawikuh. Díaz's next task was to establish a small settlement in the desert that would serve as a supply depot for the main party. He then went off to find Alarcón and his ships and carry their supplies to the depot.

Díaz and his party crossed a burning stretch of the Sonoran Desert that centuries later would be called "the Devil's Highway." When they finally reached the Gulf of California, they found no ships, only a message buried in a tree. The message was from Alarcón who had sailed back to Mexico two months earlier. Undaunted, Díaz decided to explore further north. He followed the Colorado River from near present-day Yuma, Arizona. Historians believe at some point he crossed the river and became the first European to enter what is now the state of California.

Unfortunately, Díaz did not live long enough to report on his far-flung adventures to Coronado. In a freak accident, he ran into the end of a lance he had thrown and died of his wounds a few days later. His men buried him in the wilderness and returned to Hawikuh.

The last party Coronado sent out was perhaps the most successful in fulfilling its mission. A young Indian chief visited Coronado at Hawikuh. The Spaniards named him Bigotes, Spanish for "whiskers," because he had a long mustache. Bigotes claimed to come from a pueblo to the east called Cicúye. He invited Coronado to visit him there. He also told him of a pueblo further east, called Tiguex, in the valley of the Rio Grande. Coronado may have wondered if at Tiguex he would find the cities of gold he was searching for. He sent Hernando de Alvarado and twenty men to Tiguex with Bigotes as their guide.

Alvarado was only a few miles from Hawiku when he made his first astonishing discovery. He came upon a series of crumbling fortresses and city walls that appeared to be the ruins of an unknown ancient people. Five days later, he arrived at a newer pueblo situated high atop a steep sandstone mesa more than 350 feet (107 meters) from the ground. This was Ácoma, which is still inhabited by Native Americans today. It remains the oldest continuously lived-in place in the United States.

The only entrance to Ácoma was a series of stone steps that grew narrower and narrower until they were replaced with toeholds near the top. On the summit was an arsenal of stones that the people of Ácoma could roll down upon hostile intruders.

Fortunately, they welcomed the Spaniards in friendship. "They went through their form of making peace," Castañeda wrote, "which is to touch the horses and take their sweat and rub themselves with it,

Ácoma—The Sky City

When Hernando de Alvarado arrived at Ácoma in 1540, it was already more than two hundred years old. The pueblo's location atop a steep-sided mesa made it difficult for enemies to attack it, which is why it is sometimes called "Sky City."

Although Alvarado was friendly toward the people of Ácoma, later Spanish visitors were more aggressive. Juan de Oñate entered Ácoma in 1598 and took over the pueblo. The following year the Indians revolted and were reconquered only after fierce fighting. Again in 1680, they rebelled against Spanish rule and joined the larger revolt of the Pueblo Indians in New Mexico. A third uprising in 1696 took the Spaniards three years to put down.

Today, the people of Ácoma remain proud of their long history. Visitors can watch the inhabitants make the beautiful pottery they are most famous for. Although many inhabitants remain in the original dwellings only during the day, some stay there each night, keeping secure Ácoma's claim to being the oldest continuously inhabited community in the United States.

Chosen by Native Americans for its strategic location and natural beauty, Ácoma is today a national historic landmark

and to make crosses with the fingers of the hands." The Ácoma people presented their visitors with gifts of corn bread, turkeys, and deerskins.

Alvarado stayed only a short time at Ácoma and moved on to Tiguex, located just north of present-day Albuquerque, New Mexico. The Spaniards were greatly impressed by the fertility of the soil and the region's rich, green grass that their horses feasted on.

"The country is so fertile," wrote Casteñada, "that they do not have to break up the ground the year round, but only have to sow the seeds, which is presently covered by the fall of snow, and the ears come up under the snow. In one year [they] gather enough for seven."

Alvarado was so taken with Tiguex that he sent word back to Coronado to consider making it his winter headquarters. Coronado decided to do so and began to move his army eastward.

SIX

Trouble at Tiguex

By the time Coronado and his advance party arrived at Tiguex, Alvarado had moved east to Cicúye, Bigotes's home village. The local people were overjoyed to see their chief again and threw a great celebration for him and the Spaniards.

During this time, Alvarado had a fateful meeting with a slave living among the people of Cicúye. The slave was probably a member of the Wichita or Pawnee people. The Spaniards called him "El Turco," the Turk, because he wore his hair in what looked like a Turkish turban. "The Turk" told Alvarado that there were riches to be found to the east, where he came from. He told him of a great river in which swam fish the size of horses. This land, like Cibola, had seven cities, he said. The king of each city rode in an enormous canoe with twenty paddlers on each side, he said. These kings ate their meals on gold plates and drank from golden jugs. When they sat under a large tree, tiny gold bells tin-

The Turk, named for his turban headdress, points the way to the riches of Quivira for a hopeful Coronado and his men.

kled in the afternoon breeze and lulled them to sleep. When they awoke in the hot sun, servants scraped the sweat off their skin with tiny golden blades. The name of this fabulous land was Quivira.

Alvarado believed that at last he had good news to bring back to his commander. He took the Turk with him to Tiguex. Here, the Indian told his tale to Coronado in greater detail. Coronado listened, but he remained skeptical. What proof, he demanded, did the Turk have of this land he claimed lay to the east? The Turk replied that he had bracelets of gold, but that his captors at Cicúye had taken them from him.

Alvarado was sent back to Cicúye to retrieve the bracelets. When he arrived there, Bigotes told him that the bracelets did not exist and that

El Morro's Inscription Rock

While Coronado was doing battle with the Indians at Tiguex, Tristán de Arellano was leading the main army through uncharted territory in present-day New Mexico to join him. Along the way, Arellano may have passed by one of the most incredible works of humans and nature in the Southwest.

This sandstone cliff was later named El Morro, the Spanish word for "castle" or "fort" because it resembles a castle. But its uniqueness lies in the words and figures scratched upon its face, which is known as Inscription Rock. Native Americans

Inscription Rock contains both ancient Native American petroglyphs and the names of more recent Spanish and American explorers and settlers.

had etched prehistoric drawings called petroglyphs into the soft sandstone for centuries. After Arellano passed by, it was signed by explorer and first governor of New Mexico, Juan de Oñate. His 1605 signature is the oldest recorded in North America. After him, hundreds of missionaries, soldiers, and pioneers left their names and messages on the rock.

"All who pause and ponder the messages on the wall of El Morro," wrote Stewart Udall, former United States secretary of the interior, "absorb an unutterable reverence for life and history." El Morro National Monument was established in 1906.

El Morro Bluff, also known as Inscription Rock, was a well-known landmark for pioneers and others crossing New Mexico in the eighteenth and nineteenth centuries.

the Turk was a liar. But Alvarado refused to believe his old friend. He had Bigotes and the chief elder of the village brought back to Tiguex as prisoners. The appearance in chains of these two respected leaders in Tiguex angered the natives. The winter of 1540 would not be a pleasant one.

Coronado was torn between preserving good relations with the natives and finding the wealth that he believed was still awaiting him. When one of his soldiers molested a warrior's wife, the people of the village demanded retribution. Coronado took no action. The angry villagers killed a guard and drove off the Spaniards' horses. Coronado lost his normally even temper and, in a rage, led an attack on the village where the complaint had first been made. He ordered that two hundred men be executed as an example to the others. When they realized what was to happen to them, more than one hundred of the men fled. The Spaniards managed to find and kill nearly all of them.

Feelings between the natives and the Spaniards were as cold and bitter as the winter snows that now fell on Tiguex. Coronado tried to make peace with the other eleven villages but the people wanted no more to do with him.

"It snowed so much that for the next two months it was impossible to do anything except to go along the roads to advise them to make peace. . . ." wrote Castañeda, "to all they replied that they did not trust those who did not know how to keep good faith after they had once given it."

When Cárdenas was attacked by natives with war clubs, Coronado ordered that the inhabitants of another village either surrender or suffer attack. The town did not surrender and the Spaniards held it under siege for fifty days, until the inhabitants were completely without water and they surrendered. To make amends with the Indians afterward, Coronado personally escorted the village elder back to Cicúye. He also told Bigotes that he would be released when they left to find Quivira.

The Indian towns of Cibola, Tiguex, and Quivira appear on this highly inaccurate seventeenth-century map. Note that California is shown as an island.

Coronado would lead the expedition himself and the Turk would be their guide. The Turk told Coronado not to load his pack animals with too many provisions because he would need them to carry back all the gold he would find.

SEVEN

The Sea of Grass

Once Coronado's expedition crossed the Pecos River, it entered a land such as the Spaniards had never seen before. The plains of what would one day become West Texas were covered in an endless sea of tall grass.

"Who could believe that 1,000 horses and 500 of our cows and more than 5,000 rams and ewes [female sheep] and more than 1,500 friendly Indians and scouts, in traveling over these plains, would leave no more trace where they had passed than if nothing had been there. . . ." wrote Castaneda. "The grass never failed to become erect after it had been trodden down."

Afraid those in the rear of the party would become lost, Coronado's men made piles of animal bones to mark their path.

The men soon discovered they were not alone on the plains. There were huge herds of buffalo, millions of head, which they had never seen before.

This nineteenth—century painting, set on the snow-covered plains, shows how the number of buffalo had dwindled since the days when Coronado passed here.

"They have very long beards, like goats," wrote Castañeda, describing the buffalo, "and when they are running they throw their heads back with the beard dragging on the ground . . . they have a great hump, larger than a camel's . . . they have a short tail, with a bunch of hair at the end. When they run, they carry it erect like a scorpion."

They soon met groups of Native Americans who followed the buffalo to hunt them. One of these Plains tribes were the Teyas, who later gave their name to the state of Texas. The Teyas had no horses to pur-

SPANISH HORSES, INDIAN RIDERS

The Plains Indians that Coronado encountered had no horses with which to hunt the buffalo. That changed later. Some historians believed that the horses later mastered by the Indians were the descendents of those that strayed from Coronado's expedition.

While it is true that Coronado lost many horses, there is little evidence any of them survived long enough to breed. Many of the Spanish horses died. Some were gored by herds of buffalo and others were killed in falls from rocky ravines and cliffs. None of the later Spanish explorers and settlers mention seeing any wild horses before 1700. These horses most probably were brought west by later Spaniards and adopted by the Indians. Like the legend of Cibola, the tale of Coronado's horses among the Native Americans is probably no more than an intriguing myth.

These skilful Comanche horsemen enjoyed a mobility unknown to the Native Americans Coronado encountered. Horses were not introduced to the Indians for at least 150 years after Coronado's expedition.

sue the buffalo but hunted them on foot. Their dogs dragged their belongings behind them on a travois, a device made of two poles joined by a frame. The warriors would pitch their teepees in the tall grass for days or weeks while they hunted. As Castañeda reported, they used every part of the buffalo.

> *With the skins they build their houses; with the skins they clothe and shoe themselves; from the skins they make ropes and also obtain wool. From the sinews [tendons] they make thread, with which they sew their clothing and likewise their tents. From the bones they shape awls [tools for piercing] and the dung [dried waste] they use for firewood . . . The bladders serve as jugs and drinking vessels."*

It was now the end of May and the expedition had marched more than 650 miles (1,046 kilometers) in five weeks. Food supplies were dangerously low and the men were dusty and tired. Coronado realized they would never reach Quivira under such conditions. He decided to continue with a small force of thirty horsemen and a few foot soldiers. The main party was ordered to return to Tiguex, but the men did not want to leave. Coronado compromised. He said he would send a messenger in eight days. If the news was good, he would order them to follow him to Quivira. If not, they were to return to Tiguex. With high expectations, Coronado and the small party headed north to meet their destiny.

EIGHT

End of the Rainbow

Coronado's distrust of the Turk grew daily. He had proved to be an unreliable guide, leading them aimlessly across the Texas plains. Some of the Indians they met confirmed the Turk's story about Quivira's wealth, but only after he had talked to them privately. The Teyas, whom Coronado had been careful to keep away from the Turk, only confirmed Quivira's location. They said nothing of its gold and silver. Was it possible their guide was leading them on a wild-goose chase for imaginary riches? Only time would tell. In any case, the Turk was no longer a privileged member of the expedition. He was put in chains as Coronado's prisoner until his stories proved true.

For more than a month, the party marched north through present-day Oklahoma. Then they entered what is now the state of Kansas. Here, they headed east and finally reached their long-sought goal.

The People of Quivira

The people of Quiriva were members of the Wichita tribe and were a peaceful people. They were best known for their customs of tattooing their bodies and building conical, grass-covered huts that resembled haystacks.

Although Coronado's dealings with the Wichita were friendly, they did not fare so well with later conquistadores. More than one hundred years after Coronado in 1662, Spaniard Diégo Dionisio de Pensalosa defeated the Wichita in battle, and hostile Indian tribes gradually drove them out of central Kansas into Oklahoma. There, during the 1770s and early 1800s, epidemics of smallpox killed many of them. During the American Civil War, the Wichita fled back to Kansas. The site where they settled became Kansas's largest city, Wichita, named in their honor. After the Civil War, the Wichita moved again to Oklahoma.

Today, only about two thousand Wichita remain. Most of them live on a reservation in western Oklahoma. It is a sad ending to the people on whom Coronado pinned all his hopes.

Wichita thatched lodges like this one, made of prairie grass, were kept warm by a fire within. Note the smoke rising through the central opening.

Coronado's worst fears were confirmed. Quivira had no tall towers, no glittering streets of gold. There were not even the mighty pueblos of the Zuni to greet them. Coronado had reached the end of his rainbow, and instead of a pot of gold, all that was waiting for him was a village of huts made of grass and straw. They had traveled hundreds of miles and endured endless hardships all for a clump of grass huts.

Why had the Turk tricked them? In his last interview with Coronado, the Indian guide finally told the truth. He had led Coronado astray to escape slavery and return to his people. He had also done it for the people of Cicúye. According to Castañeda, they "had asked him to lead them [the Spaniards] off onto the plains and lose them, so that the horses would die when their provisions [food] gave out, and they would be so weak if they ever returned that they could be killed without any trouble, and thus they could take revenge for what had been done to them."

This landscape by nineteenth-century American artist
George Catlin shows some of the fertile land Coronado passed
through on his way to Quivira.

Hernando de Soto – North America's Other Conquistador

While Coronado was marching towards Quivira, only a few days' journey to the east, another Spanish conquistador was also searching for gold and glory. Hernando de Soto had arrived in Florida in May 1539 and had been unsuccessfully searching the American Southeast for riches for more than two years. It is believed that Coronado had heard of de Soto's presence and sent an Indian messenger to find him, but he was unable to locate de Soto.

What would have happened if Coronado and de Soto had actually met in the heartland of America? Chances are they would have complained to each other about their failure to find the wealth that had brought them so far from home. They might have told each other about the wonders they had seen along the way. De Soto would undoubtedly have talked about the mighty Mississippi River, which he and his men were the first Europeans to see.

While both men suffered hardships, de Soto's fate was much worse. He died of fever in the summer of 1542 near Natchez, Mississippi. His men buried him in the Mississippi to keep his death a secret from the Indians. The Spaniards feared the Native Americans would kill them if they knew de Soto was dead.

The remaining members of de Soto's party wandered as far west as north Texas and then returned to the Mississippi. They followed the river down to the Gulf of Mexico and arrived at Veracruz on the Mexican coast in 1543, about a year after Coronado's return to Mexico.

Unlike Coronado, De Soto was a seasoned conquistador by the time he arrived in North America. He had earlier been part of the expedition that conquered the Incas in Peru.

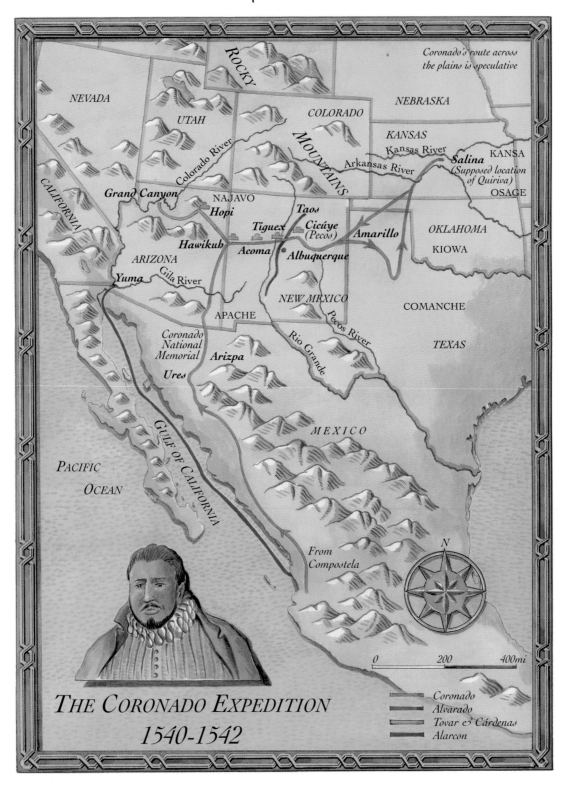

Coronado's route across the plains is speculative

THE CORONADO EXPEDITION
1540-1542

Coronado
Alvarado
Tovar & Cárdenas
Alarcon

But it was Coronado who immediately took revenge. He had two of his men drag the Turk away. They wrapped a rope around his neck and strangled him.

The party stayed in Quivira for twenty-five days. As he got to know the people of Quivira better, Coronado's disappointment faded somewhat. While Quivira had no gold, there were other riches there to be cultivated. After the party returned to Tiguex, Coronado wrote a letter to the king describing Quivira's advantages." The country itself is the best I have ever seen for producing all the products of Spain . . ." he wrote. "I found prunes like those of Spain and nuts and very good sweet grapes and mulberries."

The young soldiers agreed that the land of Kansas was fertile and well watered. It would be excellent for raising crops, cattle, and horses. "This country presents a fine appearance," wrote soldier Juan Jaramillo twenty years later. "The like of which I have not seen a better in all our Spain and Italy, not a part of France . . ." Like Coronado years earlier, these young men had nothing to look forward to back in Spain. Neither did New Spain have much to offer them. Yet in Quivira, they could stake out large estates and become wealthy landowners. They replaced one dream with another. This new dream now seemed within their grasp.

Coronado promised them that they would return to Quivira in the spring, after wintering again in Tiguex. But fate had other plans for Coronado and his expedition.

N I N E

A Conquistador's Fall

Facing another long winter in Tiguex, the Spaniards devised games and competitions to pass the time. On December 27, 1541, a feast day, a horse race was arranged between Coronado and one of his captains, Rodrigo Maldonado. Castañeda describes what happened next:

> He [Coronado] *was on a powerful horse and his servant had put on a new girth, which must have been rotten at the time, for it broke during the race and he fell over on the side where Don Rodrigo was, and as his horse passed over him it hit his head with its hoof, which laid him at the point of death, and recovery was slow and doubtful."*

The conquistador lay in a coma for days. He finally regained consciousness but felt he would not live long. He now had only one thought—to see his wife and children one last time. The rest of his men were divided on the issue of leaving Tiguex and returning to New Spain. Many of them were weary of the expedition and were ready to return home. Others were anxious to return to Quivira and start new lives on the fertile plains of Kansas.

One of the missionaries, Friar Juan de Padilla, wanted to go back to Quivira to convert and minister to the Wichita Indians. Sixty soldiers pleaded with Coronado to allow them to accompany the friar. Coronado bluntly refused. He had become suspicious and inflexible. He was no longer the noble and understanding commander they had known earlier. His head injuries may have altered his personality.

In early April 1542, the army started the long, 900-mile (1,500-kilometer) journey back to Culiacán in New Galicia. Coronado allowed Friar Juan and a small escort to return to Quivira. Friar Juan was there only a short time when a band of Indians attacked their party. The courageous friar urged the younger men with him to flee for their lives. Then he knelt in prayer and was killed by Indian arrows.

Coronado's party arrived in Culiacán in June. To his own surprise and that of his men, the conquistador had recovered from his injuries. In Culiacán, many of his men left him, scattering in several directions. Coronado continued on to Mexico City with about one hundred of the three hundred men he had started out with two years earlier.

Viceroy Mendoza was sorely disappointed that after two years of exploration, Coronado had nothing to show for his travels. Recently discovered records show Mendoza continued to support Coronado, however. Meanwhile, word spread of Coronado's bloody conflicts with the Native Americans at Hawikuh and Tiguex. The king and his officials back in Spain did not approve.

Coronado waited more than two years for Judge Lorenzo de Tejada to arrive from Spain for an official inquiry. Besides the charges against him for the fighting, Coronado was accused of having "com-

THE MIXTÓN WAR

When Coronado returned to New Spain, his province of New Galicia was recovering from a violent Indian rebellion called the Mixtón War. Coronado himself was indirectly responsible for this bloody uprising. His expedition took away many Spanish soldiers. Indian leaders took advantage of the shortage. They led an attack on the city of Guadalajara from their stronghold of the mountain village of Mixtón.

The acting governor of New Galicia was overwhelmed and appealed to Viceroy Mendoza for help. Mendoza called on friendly Aztec chieftains to lead the counterattack against the rebels. He even gave the chieftains Spanish horses to ride in the attacks. This may have been the first time the Spanish officially gave horses to the Indians.

The Spanish and their Indian allies eventually put down the uprising, but the fighting was fierce. Hernando Cortés's former lieutenant—and governor of Guatemala—Pedro de Alvarado was among the casualties. He was killed leading a foolhardy charge on the Indian town of Nochistlán.

Pedro de Alvarado's defeat at Nochistlan was a great victory for the Indians in the Mixtón War. Alvarado died from injuries when his horse fell on top of him during the battle.

In the aftermath of the Mixtón War, Mendoza may have been anxious to avoid another rebellion. He was more sensitive to Indian grievances. This may have led to some of the charges of cruelty leveled against Coronado at his trial.

ANTONIO DE MENDOZA-"THE GOOD VICEROY"

Antonio de Mendoza is considered one of the best of the Spanish administrators in the New World. He improved relations with the Indians and did much to relieve their suffering. He built schools and churches and developed both farming and industry in New Spain. Mendoza also brought the first printing press to the New World in 1535. For all these reasons, he was called "the good viceroy."

After sixteen years of service in New Spain, Mendoza was appointed viceroy of Peru in 1551. He died there the following year. Mendoza was largely responsible for laying a secure foundation for Spain's three-hundred-year rule in Mexico.

Antonio de Mendoza

mitted great cruelties upon natives of the land through which he passed." He was also charged with the death of the Turk.

The aftereffects of Coronado's head injuries left his memory fuzzy on important events, and his defense was weak. However, others from the expedition spoke up in his behalf. In the end, he was acquitted of all charges. Coronado's career in New Spain was not over, but he was removed from the post of governor of New Galicia. Thanks to Mendoza, he was elected *procurador*, a high government official, of Mexico in 1551. Yet he was never to lead another expedition of exploration.

It is not certain when Coronado died, although historians believe it was probably in September 1554. His burial place was forgotten for centuries. It was only rediscovered in the 1930s under an old church in Mexico City.

Like those of so many conquistadores before him, Francisco Vásquez de Coronado's life did not have a happy ending. The difference was that, unlike Cortés and Pizarro, Coronado had no great discovery or wealth to show for his efforts—just a wilderness of desert, rocks, and plains. However, more than 450 years later, history has changed its opinion of this ill-fated conquistador.

Afterword

Francisco Coronado may have died thinking he had lived in vain, but history says otherwise. The vast region that Coronado explored did not yield gold and silver, but it proved to have treasures more durable and lasting. Coronado and his men recognized one of those treasures—the fertile black soil of the Great Plains. Another treasure was the vast herds of buffalo that they were among the first Europeans to see. The rich grasslands of the Rio Grande Valley were still other invaluable prizes. And then there were the wonders that they didn't appreciate at the time, such as the Grand Canyon, the Colorado River, and the remarkable pueblos of the Zuni and Hopi. Coronado himself did not see all of these wonders, but without his leadership his captains would not have discovered them.

Coronado and his men never had the opportunity to return to and settle the rich land of Kansas. Yet their memory of that land and the

The buffalo was just one of the many North American wonders that Coronado and his men were probably the first Europeans to see.

pueblo peoples of the Southwest became a part of Spanish-American lore. Like his countryman Hernando de Soto, who explored the Southeast about the same time, Coronado blazed the way for later explorers, traders, and settlers. While he spilled blood in some of his confrontations with the Native Americans he met, Coronado's record among the Indians is far better than most other conquistadores's.

Archeologists have unearthed the ruins of Hawikuh, the first of the Zuni villages Coronado visited.

Perhaps what is most memorable about Coronado's achievement is the boldness of it. He led his men on an incredible three thousand-mile march into the unknown, one of the longest marches in history. That journey still fires the imagination of people today." We look for Coronado's path because he was a great, original American seeker . . ." claims writer Henry Wiencek. "[We] have learned in large part from [his] effort . . . that the very act of seeking lies at the heart of the American character."

IN THE FOOTSTEPS OF CORONADO

The memory of Coronado's expedition lived on in New Spain. It inspired later Spaniards to follow his footsteps north to this vast and unknown land of North America.

Forty years after Coronado, another expedition explored the land of Hawikuh. It brought back favorable reports of its rich grazing lands. Fifteen years later, in 1598, a colony was founded and, in 1609, it was officially named the "Kingdom of Provinces of New Mexico." A year later a capital was established called Santa Fe, which means "holy faith" in Spanish. Santa Fe remains today the oldest capital city in the United States.

In time, Arizona, Texas, and Oklahoma—all first explored by Coronado's expedition—joined New Mexico as Spanish territory in the Southwest. This territory became part of Mexico when that nation won its independence from Spain in 1821. When the United States defeated Mexico in the Mexican-American War of 1847-48, most of this region became part of the United States. However, the Spanish culture first established by Coronado more than 450 years ago lives on today in the American Southwest.

Coronado's expedition made possible the settlement of Santa Fe. The city's rich Native American past is represented by this pueblo-style hotel.

Afterword

But the last word must go to Coronado's faithful chronicler and sometime critic, Pedro de Castañeda. Although he faulted the conquistador at times for bad judgment, Castañeda also recognized that this expedition was more than a desperate search for gold and glory." It was God's pleasure," he wrote, "that these discoveries should remain for other peoples and that we who had been there should content ourselves with saying that we were the first who discovered it."

Francisco Coronado and His Times

c. 1510 Coronado is born in Salamanca, Spain.

1513 Vasco Nuñez de Balboa discovers the Pacific Ocean.

1521 Hernando Cortés conquers the Aztec Empire in Mexico.

1535 Coronado arrives in Mexico City with Viceroy Antonio de Mendoza.

1538 Coronado becomes governor of New Galicia.

1539 Friar Marcos first sees the "golden city" of Cibola.

1540 Coronado leads an expedition north to Cibola.

1541 Coronado leads a party across the American Southwest to the city of Quivira in present-day Kansas.

1542 Coronado returns to New Spain without having found gold.

1544 Coronado faces an inquiry on charges of cruelty to Indians and is acquitted.

1554 Coronado dies in Mexico City at about age forty-four.

1598 A colony is founded by Spaniards in present-day New Mexico.

1610 Santa Fe is established as the capital of the province of New Mexico.

Further Research

Books

Crisfield, Deborah and Patrick O'Brien. *The Travels of Francisco Vásquez de Coronado*. New York: Raintree Steck-Vaughn, 2001.

Doak, Robin S. *Francisco Vásquez de Coronado Explores the Southwest*. Compass Point Books, 2001.

Hossell, Karen Price. *Francisco Coronado*. Crystal Lake, Illinois: Heinemann Library, 2002.

Hurwicz, Claude. *Francisco Vásquez de Coronado*. New York: Powerkids Press, 2001.

Jacobs, William Jay. Coronado: *Dreamer in Golden Armor*. London: Franklin Watts, Inc., 1994.

Marcovitz, Hal. *Francisco Coronado and the Exploration of the American Southwest*. Broomall, Pennsylvania: Chelsea House Publishers, 2000.

Nardo, Don. *Francisco Coronado*. London: Franklin Watts, Inc., 2001.

Weisberg, Barbara. *Coronado's Golden Quest*. New York: Raintree Steck-Vaughn, 2001.

Whiting, Jim. *Francisco Vasquez De Coronado*. Bear, Delaware: Mitchell Lane Publishers, Inc., 2001.

Websites

Francisco Coronado—A Most Famous Failing
Desert USA
www.desertusa.com/mag98/sep/papr/coronado.html

Further Research

Francisco Coronado
PBS New Perspectives on the West
www. pbs.org/weta/thewest/people/a_c/Coronado.html

Francisco Vásquez de Coronado
Family Education Network
www.factmonster.com/ce6/people/A0813622.html

BIBLIOGRAPHY

Berger, Josef. *Discoverers of the New World.* New York: American Heritage Press, 1960.

Cumming, W .P, R .A. Skelton and D. B. Quinn. *The Discovery of North America.* New York: American Heritage Press, 1972.

Day, A. Grove. *Coronado's Quest: The Discovery of the Southwestern States.* Westport, Connecticut: Greenwood Publishing Group, 1982.

Castañeda, Pedro de. *The Journey of Coronado.* Mineola, New York: Dover, 1990.

Flint, Richard. *Great Cruelties Have Been Reported: The 1544 Investigation of the Coronado Expedition.* Dallas, Texas: Southern Methodist University Press, 2002.

Jensen, Malcolm C. *Francisco Coronado.* New York: Franklin Watts, 1974.

Norman, Charles. *Discoverers of America.* New York: Thomas Y. Crowell Co., 1968.

Preston, Douglas J. *Cities of Gold: A Journey Across the American Southwest.* Albuquerque, New Mexico: University of New Mexico Press, 1999.

Stein, R. Conrad. *Francisco de Coronado.* Chicago: Children's Press, 1992.

Udall, Stewart L. *To The Inland Empire: Coronado and Our Spanish Legacy.* Garden City, NY: Doubleday, 1987.

Source Notes

Chapter 2

p. 17 "to note the kind of people…" Charles Norman, *Discoverers of America*, pp. 89–90.

Chapter 3

p. 122 "The city from where I beheld it…" Josef Berger, *Discoverers of the New World*, p. 95.

Chapter 4

p. 24 "There were so many men of such high quality…" Norman, p. 95.
p. 30 "There are haciendas in New Spain…" Norman, p. 105.
p. 30 "…they knocked me down to the ground…" Norman, p. 103.
p. 31 "they are very good houses…" Norman, p. 103.
p. 31 "I can assure you that…he has not told the truth…" Norman, p. 103.

Chapter 5

p. 36 "Those who stayed above…" Norman, p. 107.
p. 37–39 "They went through their form of making peace…" Norman, p. 108.
p. 39 "The country is so fertile…" Norman, p. 108.

Chapter 6

p. 43 "All who pause and ponder…" Stewart L. Udall, *To the Inland Empire: Coronado and Our Spanish Legacy*, p. 144.
p. 44 "It snowed so much…" Norman, p. 113.

Chapter 7

p. 46 "who could believe that 1,000 horses…" Norman, p. 115.
p. 47 "They have very long beards…" Norman, p. 115.
p. 49 "With the skins they build…" Udall, p. 148.

Chapter 8

p. 52 "had asked him to lead them…" Norman, p. 118.
p. 57 "The country itself is the best I have ever seen…" Norman, pp. 119-120.
p. 57 "This country present a fine appearance…" Udall, pp. 170-172.

Chapter 9

p. 58 "He [Coronado] was on a pwerful horse . . ." Udall, p.181

pp. 59–62 "committed great cruelties upon natives…" quoted in Malcolm C. Jensen, *Francisco Coronado*, p. 52

Afterword

p. 66 "We look for Coronado's path…" Henry Wiencek. "The Spain Among Us," *American Heritage*, April 1994, p. 54.

p. 68 "It was God's pleasure…" Norman, p. 120.

INDEX

Page numbers in **boldface** are illustrations.

maps
    Coronado Expedition
        1540-1542, 56
    Indian towns, 45
    New Galicia, 15

Ácoma, 37–39, **38**
African Americans, 15
Almagro, Diego de, 9
Alvarado, Hernando de,
    37–39
Alvarado, Pedro de, 60–61
Antilia, 16–17
Arellano, Tristán de, 42–43
Arizona, 25–30, **33,** 67
Aztecs, 8–9, 60, 69

Balboa, Vasco Nuñez de, 8,
    9, 69
Bigotes, 37, 40, 41–44
buffalo, 46–47, **47, 65**

Cabeza de Vaca, Álvar
    Núñez, 17
California, 21, 36–37, **45**
Cárdenas, García Lopez de,
    32–36
Castañeda, Pedro de, 24,
    44, 46, 58, 68
charity, 16
Charles I (king of Spain),
    10, **10,** 11
conquistadors, 8, 66
Coronado, Francisco **16,**
    25
    birth, 9, 69
    career, 11–16, 62–63, 69

death, 63, 69
finances, 11, 12
friends, 11
importance, 6–7, 64–67
injuries, 31, 58–59, 62
marriage, 12
personality, 16, 59
trial, 59–62, 69
Cortés, Hernando, 8–9, 14,
    14, 22–23, 69

dates, 69
desert, 36
De Soto, Hernando, 54–55,
    55
Díaz, Melchior, 36–37

El Morro, **42,** 42–43, **43**
Escalante, Francisco, 34
Estéban, 17–22
expeditions
    Cibola, **7,** 22–31, **56**
    Quivira, 46–59, **51,**
        52–53, 56

Florida, 17, 54–55

gold, 9, 22, 40–41
Grand Canyon, 32–36, **33,**
    35
Guzmán, Nuño de, 15

Hopi, 32
horses, 48, 60

Inscription Rock, **42,**
    42–43, **43**

journals, 24, 44, 46, 58, 68
Kansas, 50–57, 69

Mendoza, Antonio de
    (viceroy), 11–12, **13,**
    17, 22, 59, 60–62, **62**
Mexican American War, 67
Mexico, 8–9, 15–16
Mexico City, 12, 14
missionaries, 20–21, 59
Mixtón War, 60–61, **61**

Native Americans, 12,
    15–16, 44, **45,** 52, 59
    See also Ácoma; Hopi;
        Mixtón War;
        Pawnees; Pueblos;
        Teyas; Wichitas;
        Zuñi
New Galicia, **15,** 15–16
New Mexico, 30, 38, 39, **42,**
    42–43, **43,** 67, **67,** 69
Niza, Friar Marcos de,
    17–22, 23, 27–31, 69

Oklahoma, 50, 67
Onate, Juan de, 38
orphanages, 16

Pacific Ocean, 8, **9,** 69
Padilla, Juan de, 59
Pawnees, 40
Peru, 9, 14
petroglyphs, **42,** 42–43
Philip II (king of Spain), 10
Pizarro, Francisco, 9
Pueblos, 38

Index

Quivira, 46–57, **51,** 69
rivers, 32–37, **33,** 40

Salamanca, 9–11
Serra Junípero, Miguel, 21,
    21
Seven Cities of Cibola, 6, 14,
    16–22, 31, 69
ships, 23, 33, 36
slaves, 15
    See also the Turk

Sonoran Desert, 36
South America, 9
Spain, 8–10
supplies, 23, 27, 33, 36,
    49

Texas, 17, 46–49, 67
Teyas, 47–49, 50
Tovar, Pedro de, 32
The Turk, 40–41, **41,** 45,
    50, 52–57, 62

United States, 67

Websites, 70–71
Wichitas, 40, 51, **51**

Zuñi, 18–22, **19, 26–27,**
    28–31, **29, 66**